KOKOSCHKA

PHAIDON

I. Self-Portrait. 1912. Detail from Plate 11

KOKOSCHKA

BY LUDWIG GOLDSCHEIDER
IN COLLABORATION WITH THE ARTIST

WITH FIFTY COLOUR PLATES

PUBLISHED BY THE PHAIDON PRESS

PLATES PRINTED BY V · S · K PRINTERS · BASLE

TEXT PRINTED BY HUNT BARNARD & CO · LTD · AT THE SIGN OF THE DOLPHIN

AYLESBURY · BUCKINGHAMSHIRE · ENGLAND

A Colloquy Between
OSKAR KOKOSCHKA
and Ludwig Goldscheider
Villeneuve : 1962

A SUNNY DAY IN DECEMBER, *Christmas still a fortnight away. The sky is green, as in Bruegel's winterscape; soon there will be snow again. Rime crusts the path that leads up from Lake Geneva to the artist's home. At a distance: a farmstead, almost merging into the landscape. Close up: a small structure of finest proportions – a work of art.*

The master awaits his guest at the lattice-gate. The head of a peasant! At close quarters: the face of an aged monk, obsessed by but a single thought. I know it well, this face, yet am surprised anew every time I behold it. It is so utterly different from the faces of all other painters.

Inside too the house is unlike the abode of a painter. No vast studio to which sparse living quarters are appended, almost as though by default. The entire house here is in the service of everyday life. There is nothing ostentatious about the small room, called 'the library', which is reserved for the painter's work. Here art comes into being, straight from the very life of a man, as it happens to be lived, day after day – art that urges back into life.

Only three works are in sight on this particular day, a tapestry and two unfinished paintings. Compared with this tapestry, 'Amor and Psyche', all that the French have done in this medium over the past several decades pales into insignificance. The weaving is incredibly fine and faithful, the figures are as large as Raphael's in the Vatican tapestries. The two paintings on their easels, a 'Herodotus' and an 'Abduction', conjure up the lost art of Greek painting. Their tints carry the solemn, burning luminosity of autumn foliage, or of Japanese lanterns shining in the night.

In the presence of these great, glowing figures it is impossible to keep one's mind on talk. Their contemplation would command all one's resources. The painter and his guest move to the adjoining room and sit down.

OK: Tell me, old friend, how do you like my new paintings?

LG: Magnificent! Not only better than anything to be seen about, at the shows in Vienna, Paris, London, New York – but I like them even better than the classical compositions you painted yourself ten years ago. Your new pictures are simpler and more monumental. One would have to show your 'Herodotus' beside the 'Jeremiah' on the Sistine ceiling, to demonstrate how closely related they are.

OK: Please, please! Stop comparing me with such demi-gods – you make me blush! Tell me honestly, do you really think my work has become better? I often hear a different opinion.

LG: You mean what the critics said about your recent great Autumn Show in the Tate Gallery? You don't really expect that one can praise Matthieu and Moreni, frottage and collage, tachism and automatism – and still have any appreciation left for such paintings as your 'Herodotus'?

OK: All right, all right – but did you read what one of those critics said about me in one of the London art journals? First of all, I have no sense of design or line whatever, I don't know how to put paint on canvas – except perhaps in my earliest pictures. My two large triptychs 'do not succeed', he says, and the only things that are really good are a number of my landscapes. But 'when they don't work (those landscapes), or when the spectator cannot screw himself up into a mood of intense receptivity, they look like nothing on earth, save perhaps a Fair Isle pullover run up by a tipsy knitter.' That's what he says!

LG: Calls himself a critic and helps to shape public opinion! Well, works from a painter's maturity, with their simplifications and form resolutions, have always been poorly received. It's not so very long ago people first began to realize that the works of Rembrandt's last ten years are of much greater stature than his earlier ones. And I think Alfred Neumeyer – who has written about you too, as you know – is the only one who, as early as 1930, maintained that Michelangelo's last frescoes are better than his first. The other critics marked them down as a sad decline, a 'kind of mannerism'. Well, that's the stage you have now reached with your critics. Adolf Loos was right, when he called you 'the greatest painter of the future' fifty years ago. The pictures you painted fifty years ago now enjoy the full light of recognition and admiration. The later ones will have to wait for *their* fiftieth birthday before everyone understands their significance. But even today it isn't as though there were complete ignorance of how your works rank. Wingler, for example, wrote – here, let me read it to you: 'What will determine the verdict of history is that the promise of his brilliant opening notes was fulfilled in the mature works of his old age, in which Kokoschka is drawing the balance of all his insight and experience. His power of transforming the inner substance of his mind into pictorial terms has grown with the years.' That's what *Wingler* says, and he's right!

OK: You make me blush like a young girl! Unfortunately, most of the rest put it differently.

LG: And how long do you think they'll have anything to say? You'll do better to listen to the voices of poets and creative writers. They won't fade quite so fast – Karl Kraus, Else Lasker-Schüler, Albert Ehrenstein, Rainer Maria Rilke, Thomas Mann – they have all written about you and praised you as only a great painter can be praised. You should be well pleased!

OK: I am indeed, I have no complaint. If they'll just let me paint! I paint as well as I can, I paint all the time, I love to paint, and I take my time. How long would you guess I've been painting on those two pictures?

LG: Didn't I see them up on those easels during my last visit, three years ago?

OK: It's at least as long as that, and I'm still not finished with them.

LG: But the pictures have changed in the meantime. The head of Herodotus is turned now, and the way the abductor stands, lifting up the heavy female figure, is quite different. Your figures seem to be forever turning on coil springs, until the pressure lets up at last and they become fixed – just as in Michelangelo's drawings . . .

OK: Please, please! Keep those sacred names out of it!

LG: . . . where a single body sometimes has to try on its arms in seven positions, the head shown first turned to the left, then to the right, once inclined and again raised. The whole thing twangs like a coil spring. But tell me, why didn't you make three different versions of 'The Abduction'? It would have taken no more time, and we would have had more out of it.

OK: Ah, my dear friend, I couldn't do such a thing. I just don't paint that way. With me a painting has to grow on the canvas. I ask myself how solid bodies must be placed in space, in the depths of space. I have to shift them back and forth until I get it right. Sometimes I do a pencil sketch, but only to record an idea. I never make a proper outline on the canvas. It wouldn't serve any purpose. I know what I'm after – the whole painting is finished in my head. I look at my canvas and try to project it. I see the entire thing before me, and I must never lose too much of it. I must get it on the canvas as I have it in my head, I paint layer upon layer, and if I don't capture it at once as I see it before me, I paint it over – that's why my paint is sometimes so thick. That doesn't matter. The only important thing is that the pigments don't get dirty, for spatial depth can only be reproduced through the luminosity of the colours.

LG: Is it true to say that you learned this technique while painting landscapes?

OK: Could be. All I know is that I used in my landscapes the techniques I learned in painting portraits.

LG: Just what do you mean by technique? Do you mean composing in colour?

OK: No, I mean everything! The colour part and the graphic element, the placement of solid bodies in space, the gradations of light and dark, the arrangement of all the pictorial elements in one plane without losing spatial depth.

LG: Spatial depth – since when has that seemed of such importance to you? The story goes that Klimt and Japanese wood-cuts influenced you in your beginnings. They avoid spatial depth, they are two-dimensional.

OK: That's not quite true. Japanese wood-cuts do contain space, though expressed by uniform colour surfaces, achieving depth like stage flats; and there's space in Klimt's drawings and paintings too, except when he becomes completely decorative, and there he holds no interest for me. What I did learn from the Japanese, by the way, is something altogether different from arrangements in a plane or good taste in colour. The French pinched that from them. What I learned from them is rapid and precise observation of movement. The Japanese have the sharpest eyes in the whole history of painting. Every horse in their pictures jumps properly; every butterfly settles correctly on its petal; every wood-cutter swings his adze as he should; indeed, every movement of man and beast is accurately reproduced. Movement! But movement exists only in space, in three-dimensional space. That's what I learned from the Japanese. And then I found that isn't enough. Painting, you know, isn't based on just three dimensions, but on four. The fourth dimension is a projection of myself. There's a big world of which I actually know nothing. And there's a small world, my world. It's a projection of myself, the fourth dimension. The other three dimensions are based on the vision of both eyes (not just one); the fourth dimension is based on the essential nature of vision, which is creative. And I think that's the way the Greeks thought of it too. The Greek world is a projection beyond the individual self, it's an indestructible world of its own, quite different from any other we know – Babylon, Mexico, India, the Gothic Age in Europe, etc. That's true of painting, of sculpture, of architecture, of literature, of science – of everything. The Greeks created their own world by projecting their vision and their nature as men, enormously magnified. The Bible is another powerful projection of a people and its character. All the characters in the Bible are enlarged symbols of all the opportunities for growth that are open to man.

LG: As I apprehend your art, it has been drawing all its power, for forty years, solely from the world of Greece. But what about the Bible? You've sometimes brushed it in passing, but you've never made the stories and figures of the Bible your own. Why? You who unlike any painter since the Renaissance understands both the kinship and the hostility between the worlds of Greece and of the Bible! Why don't you paint the prophets and the evangelists, as you have painted Prometheus and Herodotus?

OK: Ah – life is too short! You see how long it all takes. The long time needed to solve even the problem of bringing order into so many planes in one picture, all oriented in different directions. Take 'The Abduction' here. How is this Delphi to be intertwined with the background colours? How is one to make the two main figures come out monumental in aspect, so that they may be seen on their own – even though they exist only in concert with all else in the picture? How long it took me to master merely the techniques of painting! Without technique one can do nothing – one cannot play music, build, fence, dance, paint – especially paint. And the technique of vision must be mastered even before one tries to learn to paint. Life is too short, it passes too swiftly. It isn't so very long ago that I was eighteen. Since that time I have only just learned how to do properly what I want to do. I know I'll get done with those two paintings here – but I'm not finished yet, and the years are slipping by.

LG: You've painted something like four or five hundred pictures by now. Rembrandt didn't do very many more. There are also your water colours, stage designs, drawings, lithographs, illustrations for your own books and others. True, many years have gone by, but you've made good use of the time you had. You needed only a few hours for some of your paintings, and many years for others. Your portrait of Masaryk took more than a year, that of the Countess of Drogheda three or four years, 'Amor and Psyche' five years, 'The Spring' longest of all, fifteen years, with few interruptions.

OK: Yes, yes – and if I still had the picture in my studio, I would still be painting on it – it still isn't quite as I'd like it to be.

LG: What were the difficulties you had with that picture?

OK: Technical problems. All the things I call 'technique'. The picture I had in my head and the one on the canvas are not identical. My technique gave out. Within me the picture was marvellous, but you need technique to project the whole thing, not merely parts of it – to make everything quite clear, just as you see it before your eyes, whether it has grown slowly or all of a sudden.

LG: When you say 'before your eyes', do you mean it in the sense that one sees things in nature?

OK: Yes – that too. The things I see outside, and what is visible within me. A picture is a projection.

LG: It is right to say that a true artist doesn't imitate nature but rather nature's creative process?

OK: A painter doesn't copy anything, he makes a picture. A picture is something that wasn't there before, you have to *make* it. A picture has to derive from a phenomenon that amazed me, terrified me, opened my eyes wide, and I must keep them open to master the phenomenon. You 'make yourself a picture', and when you have it, it gives you a fright. The terror is in the picture just as it was in the phenomenon before.

LG: What you have just said explains to me why your pictures always surprise and startle me over again, whenever I see them, even when I think I know them by heart. At your last London show the pictures I know best startled me most – 'The Power of Music', 'The Portrait of the Marabout', the 'Thermopylae triptych'. With what impetus these pictures are painted! They are painted with the whole arm, the whole body, not just a hand and the fingers. That's the way the aged Tintoretto painted, and the aged Rembrandt – no, don't argue with me, let me finish! Even their contemporaries – whether they esteemed the art or not – realized that these late paintings and drawings by Michelangelo and Tintoretto were made *in furore*, at white heat. That means passion rather than sketchiness. Every stroke of the brush is final, stands as immutably as each tone in a symphony, each word in a great poem. The oddest thing about your painting is that the sheer physical energy contained in the brush strokes has grown with the years. Such an increase in impetus and in the power of vision and of recording is seen elsewhere only in masters I must not mention nor compare with you, since it makes you impatient.

OK: Of course it makes me nervous, when you keep mentioning me in the same breath with these giants – it makes me feel like a pygmy. My paintings can't stand the strong light that shines on the works of these demi-gods. For fifty years, on my knees, I have carefully studied the mature works of Titian, Tintoretto and Rembrandt, and I know them too well to imagine I belong anywhere in their company. Off with you, old friend – that's nothing but flattery, which I don't want and don't need. I'm quite content if people give only a few minutes to my pictures. Just let them look, quietly.

LG: I don't say it to ingratiate myself with you, I say it to ventilate a profound experience. It is a strain to look at your pictures – it destroys resistance, exhausts me utterly. Two hours at your show, and I was as tired as though I'd gone on some wild adventure, passed a difficult examination.

OK: But some of the important pictures weren't even there.

LG: What was there was rich enough, and beautiful enough. At any rate, there was much more to see at the London show than at the Vienna show seven years before. That was a good show, by the way. The only silly one was the exhibition of drawings, right after the war, at the *Neue Wiener Galerie*, under the title of 'Klimt, Schiele and Kokoschka'.

OK: I was an admirer of Klimt, and when I was twenty he bought some of my drawings. Mine looked a little like his, because they too were austerely linear, without shading – the lines not as pure as his, but broken and less uniform. Yet in one major aspect they were quite different: Klimt always showed his nudes standing or seated, always completely at rest; while I then drew only nudes *in action*, the movements caught in a flash – I learned that from the Japanese. I actually met and spoke to Klimt only once, at the first *Kunstschau*. I never visited his studio.

LG: And what about Schiele, your other partner in that Vienna show of 1945?

OK: Oh yes – him I have had to drag about with me, ever since he exhibited his drawings side by side with mine, at the second *Kunstschau*. The point was always made that his linear style derived from Klimt, yet his drawings were time and again compared with mine, as though there were even the slightest resemblance. When Schiele died at twenty-eight, one of the art dealers bought up everything he had left, and then he wrote a book on Schiele, which people still read.

LG: That was Dr Nirenstein. There were others in Vienna who championed Schiele, such as Werner Hofmann, now director of the Museum of the Twentieth Century. Hofmann spoke of Schiele's 'genius as a draughtsman'.

OK: All people are born with genius. All children are inspired artists. That discovery was made by Franz Cižek, who ran a course for children at the *Kunstgewerbeschule*. There were hundreds of young geniuses in his classes, but not one of these children became a painter. A child is born with eyes, but what he has to learn is how to use them properly. Every human being is endowed with genius at birth, the only question is why most of them lose this gift so quickly, or why it is withdrawn from them. Schiele always had swarms of girls about him, women, hangers-on, it began even when he was still at the academy. They were his undoing. Klimt too drew women, for the most part; but he was a true artist. His nudes are very beautiful, pure contour – he worked like that because he was so taken with Rodin's drawings.

LG: Actually, this linear style is nothing new. The engraved figures on Greek mirror covers are in this style, as are the engraved drawings on Etruscan bronze cists. Genelli and Flaxman drew like that, and later Maillol and Matisse.

OK: True enough – but my early drawings weren't quite like that. My models were children of acrobats, skinny and lean – I drew them in plain pencil lines, but *always in space, always in motion,* never calligraphically. And always from life. When I began to teach at the *Kunstgewerbeschule* – at night, by day I was still a student – we continued to draw from such models, these emaciated children, five-minute sketches, closely observed, bones, movements as precise as possible. Later my method of action drawing was introduced in all the art schools. The only reason these models, thin as a rail, suited me was because they showed joints, muscles and sinews so plainly and expressed every movement far more strongly than do plumper models. Another thing, a small marble figure by Georges Minne, shown at the second *Kunstschau,* made a tremendous impression on me: 'Kneeling Boy'. Minne must have had models as skinny as my circus children. I can see his 'Kneeling Boy' before me today – after more than fifty years.

LG: I think I know that piece. Dr Fritz Wärndorfer in Vienna had a whole collection of Minne sculptures, including a 'Kneeling Boy'.

OK: It was from Minne that I took over a preference for these fleshless young Gothic bodies. I was the first to show such models to the students and have them draw from them. For the rest, the entire Vienna *Kunstgewerbeschule* was oriented towards ornamentation. Nothing but weeds and flowers and tendrils writhing about like worms. To draw the human figure was taboo. Of course I rebelled against that.

LG: Wasn't there a painting class and a life class at the *Kunstgewerbeschule?*

OK: A painting class – that was much later, after my time. Nudes were only drawn on the side, so to speak, actually painted, in tempera and in large size, stylized as much as possible. Black and white, sometimes a bit of red or terracotta. I just didn't want to go along. I said to Czeschka – he was my teacher and made me his assistant after two years – I can't do it, it bores me! I can't paint anyone life-size so far away, I can hardly see the model. I've always been near-sighted, and I still am today.

LG: But what about your *Die Traumtragenden* ('The Dream Bearers')? Weren't they life-size nudes, painted in tempera?

OK: Life-size, yes. And in tempera too. But with heavy outlines, in several colours, without shading. A huge picture. The *Kunstgewerbeschule* provided the canvas, and the paints as well. I couldn't have afforded it. That was in 1908, an important year for me. I was working for the *Wiener Werkstätte* at the time, designing postcards and bookplates and painting fans, all for a few shillings – I was very poor. I turned out everything they asked of me – and I soon was fed up with it, I can tell you. At just the right moment Loos, the great Vienna architect, entered my life, like a fairy king in one of Raimund's magic plays. He had faith in my talent and helped get me out of the *Kunstgewerbeschule,* and soon afterwards I got rid of the *Wiener Werkstätte* as well. Its founder, Josef Hoffmann, had introduced me there in 1907, and it was his idea too that I should paint fans. I painted them with figures rather than ornaments, as was perhaps desired. They weren't at all bad, those fans. No one knows where they are now. Almost everything I did for the *Wiener Werkstätte* is lost. Even *Die Traumtragenden* belonged to it, it lay about somewhere, rolled up in three parts. Loos wanted to buy it, but it couldn't be found. I'd love to see that picture again – I don't quite remember how it looked, probably something like the lithographs for my first book, 'The Dreaming Youths', which the *Wiener Werkstätte* printed in 1908. I was proud of my first printed book – and I'm still proud today

II. St. Stephen's Cathedral, Vienna. Detail from Plate 46

III. Country House of the Gem-Dealer Rossi. Design for a stage set. 1959. In the artist's possession

whenever my work is printed. That same year the *Wiener Werkstätte* also printed the 'Hunt Book' (*Jagdbuch*) – framework and ornaments were by Löffler, I drew in the figures. The best thing I did for the *Wiener Werkstätte* – and who knows where it is today? – was something for Eleonora Duse, who was making a guest appearance in Vienna. She was perhaps the most famous actress in all of Europe – only Sarah Bernhardt was still more famous, and she was then past sixty-five. It was the time when Duse was having her love affair with d'Annunzio, and she was appearing in one of his plays, the title role in *La Gioconda* at the *Burgtheater*. 'We must do something for Duse,' Josef Hoffmann told me. 'We must make a beautiful binding for all d'Annunzio's books for her. Would you like to do it?' I had learned bookbinding, printing, lithography at the *Kunstgewerbeschule*, indeed, almost every possible craft. 'Yes,' I said, and was happy. 'What kind of material will you use?' 'Parchment.' 'Very well,' he said, 'but parchment is quite expensive – you'll have to watch your step. How will you go about it?' 'Pyrography,' I said. I knew I could do it, and we had a pyrography set at the school. Then I made a few drawings. (I'd love to see them again – they must have been quite good – Hoffmann, at least, liked them very much.) All this was before 'The Dreaming Youths'. I got the commission through the *Kunstgewerbeschule*, though actually through Josef Hoffmann, who was associated with both the *Kunstgewerbeschule* and the *Wiener Werkstätte*. In both these institutions I was the only one who drew *only* figures, I never fell for the vogue for ornamental decoration. Josef Hoffmann was right in the middle of it, he had just designed the decorations for Klimt's studio in the Feldmühlgasse, all in the geometric style, nothing but squares and oblongs. Loos didn't have to tell me anything about his crusade against ornament, I never had any taste for it, no more than for abstract art today. It's all unhuman. I covered the parchment bindings of the six or eight d'Annunzio books with figure drawings, all the lines burned in, uniform and black. I had the privilege of presenting them to La Duse in person. That was my finest day.

LG: Did you make any other bindings?

OK: I'm not quite sure any more. The binding of Löffler's 'Hunt Book', leather, with a stag embossed on the front, that's one I did.

LG: And then the binding for 'The Dreaming Youths' and the 'Four Plays'.

OK: 'The Dreaming Youths' is entirely my own work, even the script. It was Larisch who taught me lettering. The words closely set, without capitals – that was his idea. He joined the *Kunstgewerbeschule* during my third year there, a fine fellow, I was very fond of him.

LG: You were at the *Kunstgewerbeschule* for five years in all. What did you do when you finally cut loose?

OK: I was free only from the Autumn of 1909 to the Spring of 1911, then I had to take over an evening course at the *Kunstgewerbeschule* again. The time in between was filled with an immense amount of work. Mainly portraits, in Vienna and in Switzerland – the kind that were later called 'psychological portraits'.

LG: Shouldn't they rather be called 'physiognomic portraits'? – I mean physiognomic in the sense of Lavater and the young Goethe.

OK: They have been called all sorts of things – clairvoyant, hallucinatory, caricatures, and I don't know what else!

LG: They're certainly no caricatures. What they are is precisely physiognomic. When *Zeit im Bild* in 1913 published a caricature of Karl Kraus and he protested against this distortion of his features in *Die Fackel*, he said: 'My vanity, which does not extend to my body, would gladly recognize itself in a monster, if it recognized therein the spirit of the artist. I am proud of the testimony of a Kokoschka, because the truth of a distorting genius rises above anatomy, and before art reality is but an optical illusion.' I think this is important, in view of the insistence that expressionist portraiture is akin to caricature. It is overlooked, by the way, that in your portraits colour is as expressive as form.

OK: What the mission of colour is in a portrait I knew long before the first Kraus portrait. The earliest of all my portraits, which holds everything I then wanted to do and was able to do, is the portrait of Lotte Franzos. The girl was very close to me and I was extremely fond of her. That is why I suddenly knew how I had to paint her. I painted her like a candle flame: yellow and transparent light blue inside, and all about, outside, an aura of vivid dark blue. She was the first woman I painted and the first who loved me. She loved not just my painting but me, myself – she wanted to help me in everything. She was all gentleness, lovingkindness, understanding. She chose me – because of her femininity. I didn't understand that until much later. Perhaps she herself didn't quite understand it. She didn't quite know what to do with me. Soon afterwards I painted the mountains in Switzerland – I didn't understand them either. But when I painted the *Dent du Midi*, I was fortunate, just as I was with Lotte Franzos. I painted the landscape in the same colours as the portrait, warm and light, but what a light there is in that snowscape! The impressionists wouldn't have been able to do such a thing, they have an altogether different idea of light – how the *eye* is struck by sunbeams and reflections – while here it is *sensibility* on which light impinges, it's a spiritual light, a light as of the morning, the morning of life. Only there can one feel light like that. With this landscape, and this portrait of a woman, I staked out my conquest of painting. A light was kindled for me. At this same time some drawings I had published in the Berlin periodical *Der Sturm* attracted much notice among a small circle of artists and connoisseurs. Especially the four drawings for my play 'Murder Hope of Women'. I wrote the piece in 1907, made the drawings in 1908, and text and drawings were printed in *Der Sturm* in 1910. What irritated people particularly was that the nerves were drawn outside the figures, on the skin, as though they could in fact be seen. There was a good reason why I did it in this way – it came from experience, so to speak. The play printed in *Der Sturm* had already been performed in the *Gartentheater* during the first *Kunstschau*. I directed it myself and even made up all the actors. The Greeks put masks on their actors, to fix character – sad, passionate, angry, etc. I did the same thing in my own way, by painting on faces, not as decoration, but to underline the character. It was all meant to be effective at a distance, like fresco painting. All I was after was this enhancement of expression. I treated the members of the cast quite differently. Some of them I gave cross stripes, like a tiger or a cat, but I painted the nerves on all of them. Where they are located I knew from my study of anatomy, for we even studied anatomy at the *Kunstgewerbeschule*. There was a mad doctor who taught the subject, he was a very good teacher. Organs, joints, muscles, nerves – how they are constructed, how they function – it all interested me very much, because I always had some ache or pain. I was indifferently dressed then, protected neither against the heat in the summer nor the cold in winter, and I didn't eat enough either. The money my parents gave me for lunch I spent on books. The winters were quite severe, and I wouldn't wear an overcoat. I was more interested in locating the nerves that hurt me than in being more considerate of myself. During my time at the *Kunstgewerbeschule* I often didn't get home until early in the morning. My poor mother stayed up to give me hot milk. This was kept from my father. He always left the house very early in the morning, to arrive in time at his place of business, a jeweller's shop in the city, where he worked as bookkeeper into his advanced age. I caused my mother much grief in those years of my beginnings. But I had a difficult time myself. I always sensed my own nerves and that's why I painted them on the actor's skins. I made them show on all the figures in my early drawings as well. The readers of *Der Sturm*, of course, didn't know the reason. They thought these little crooked pen strokes, looking like the roots of plants, were only a quirk of mine.

LG: When you came back to Vienna from Berlin and *Der Sturm*, did your friendship with Lotte Franzos continue?

OK: Yes, but not for very long. You see, I already knew Alma Mahler. One day she came up to my studio – my mother had rented a small studio for me, in the Stubenring, not far from the *Kunstgewerbeschule*. Alma Mahler just knocked on the door, and there she was, inside. Lotte Franzos stood at her easel, painting. Alma didn't say a single word, nothing – she just packed up Lotte's easel, and everything else that belonged to her, and threw it all out. Lotte Franzos went off, and I never saw her again, except once, in a hospital in America, where she died of cancer, poor thing.

LG: So Alma Mahler followed Lotte Franzos. That association lasted for almost three years. You owe much to Alma – some of your finest paintings, especially 'The Tempest'.

OK: I painted 'The Tempest' from memory, when I had already separated from Alma Mahler. I don't much like to think back to that time, except for the trip to Naples and Venice we shared. A marvellous experience! Yes, those pictures by the Venetian masters – they opened my eyes wide – Veronese, Titian – such colours, such freedom! And, best of all, Tintoretto! It was tremendously exciting. I saw how one really ought to paint.

LG: Yet every new period of yours begins with landscapes, and in the first years following your Italian journey you painted very few landscapes – almost nothing but portraits, all of them with strangely asymmetrical faces.

OK: Yes – I got that from Scopas. He's the most interesting of the later Greek sculptors – he was active from about 370 to 340 B.C., after the wars with Sparta, when Athens was already finished, no more work on the Acropolis, the artists moving away in swarms. Scopas. was among them – he always attracted my notice, though there isn't much left today that can be attributed to his hand with certainty. There's a marble head in Vienna, that's by him, and in Dresden there's the cast of a head, of which I think I've now seen the original in Athens. The reliefs from the Temple of Athena in Tegea in Arcadia are there too. These heads are asymmetrical – I took a close look at them. Of course we had plaster casts at the high school, from which I graduated before joining the *Kunstgewerbeschule*; but those heads were from sculptures of the classical period, austerely symmetrical. This symmetry never convinced me. The two sides of a face just can't be identical, I told myself. Scopas was a naturalist – he made his heads as *portraits*, and in a portrait the two sides of a face must always be different. That's the way to do portraits, I said to myself, but the two aspects must be 'meshed', so that the transition is imperceptible. I owe that to Scopas. I learned how to use my eyes from him.

LG: And why is it that all the people of whom you made portraits look so old? From whom did you learn that? In all your drawings and paintings of Alma Mahler she looks like a woman *entre deux âges*.

OK: Well, first of all Mme Mahler was seven years older than I – that's quite important when one is still young; and another thing: the portrait painter who observes all the features in a face and reinforces them in his likeness merely brings out what time itself will later bring out. I have been told quite often: 'The portrait you painted of me grows more like me with every passing year.' Alma Mahler hadn't the least idea of life and its vicissitudes – all she knew about was love, and opera.

LG: If a monument is ever erected to her – after all, she is the authoress of a remarkable autobiography – it should bear four allegorical figures: music, painting, architecture, literature. You yourself could serve as model for the Allegory of Painting.

OK: It's no laughing matter. For me this was the most unquiet time of my life. I disentangled myself from her in the Spring of 1914, but it still wasn't quite finished, and when the war broke out a few months later I enlisted and joined the army soon afterwards. After I was seriously wounded at the front, I was put in a military hospital, first in Vienna, then in Dresden. I never heard anything further from Alma Mahler. She was married to Gropius, a union that didn't last very long. If it's true that he was jealous of me, well, he didn't have any reason, for I began a new life in Dresden. I gathered new friends about me, it was a happy time, despite the dreadful pain from the war injury, which lasted for years.

LG: In Dresden you began to paint marvellous, spacious landscapes, the first bright and appealing landscapes since your first Swiss journey. You did figure compositions too, in the same format and colours as your landscapes. Some of these paintings have an element of pathos, but all of them also have an element of joy. There is no sign that the painter of these pictures was ill and suffering pain – perhaps you were already on the way to recovery. The war was over and you stayed in Dresden, as a professor at the Academy. This went on until 1924.

OK: Yes, and then came the time of my great journeys.

LG: Seven years. The most beautiful of all your landscapes dates from this period – the large view of Chamonix. – Three times a new era in your life began in Switzerland: in 1910, when you painted the 'Dent du Midi' and the 'Portrait of Auguste Forel' – that was when you discovered the expressive values of colour; in 1927, when you painted 'Lac d'Annecy' and 'Chamonix: Montblanc' – that was when you annexed the depths of space, the third dimension, to your painting; and something further happened in 1953, after you finally settled in Switzerland: you conquered the fourth dimension – what you call 'projection' – and the movement of bodies in space became the most important element in your pictures.

OK: Yes, there's truth in that. Yet the 'thirteen years of flight' played a greater role in my life than the 'seven years of great journeys'. Since the hour of the founding of the Third Reich – an event that found a resounding echo in Austria – I knew that there was no more place for me in my homeland. I went to Prague, where lived my beloved sister, who was ill. She was a talented poet; and she made a fine relief portrait of myself, now executed in china by the Berlin Porcelain Manufactory. Spied on by the Nazis on my account, she was later denied an exit visa by the Communists as well, when she tried to join me abroad. She died in Prague, ill and alone, terrified by her environment. My years in Prague really amounted to exile, yet it was a good time. I shall never forget my talks with Masaryk. What made us friends was that we both admired the humanist-philanthropist teachings of the baroque philosopher Amos Comenius. In Prague I found other people who became dear to me, above all Olda Palkovska, who grew to be everything to me – conscience, solace, memory, wife. In Germany, at the time, a published collection of my drawings was burned, my pictures were removed from the museums and confiscated from private collections; they were exhibited as examples of 'degenerate art' and mocked. And then came the dreadful war years, years of humiliation and deprivation in London, sorrow over the death of friends and strangers, concern over the fate of Europe. I found people in London whom I had known before, and in Scotland I found mountain landscapes that warmed my heart. I worked almost ceaselessly during those years, I wrote essays, I painted flowers and figures, since I was not allowed to paint landscapes unless I submitted them to the censor, which I found unacceptable. Even shows of my work were resumed after the war – there were exhibitions in Holland, America, Switzerland. In 1953 I moved to Switzerland; and that same year I founded the 'School of Seeing' in Salzburg. Ever since the Greeks, art has been a language capable of communicating a more immediate knowledge than the spoken word. The language of pictures springs from the vision of creative man. In articulate form it becomes a message of common humanity beyond eons. The 'School of Seeing' is meant as a place of refuge before the iconoclast assault that today calls itself 'non-objective art'.

LG: It is strange how relentlessly you fought against ornament in your youth, even though the hotbeds of ornamentation, the *Kunstgewerbeschule* and the *Wiener Werkstätte*, welcomed you with open arms. Today you acknowledge only visual and representational art, while you uncompromisingly reject 'abstract art', and indeed all movements in art that dogmatically demand alienation from the reality of the world image. Yet these 'modern' movements, on their part, have always accepted you and your art. First there was *Der Sturm* in Berlin, where your work was shown beside that of Kandinsky and Klee; then there was the Dada movement in Zurich, where even your plays were performed, and *La Révolution Surréaliste* in Paris welcomed you as a contributor, beside Arp, Braque and Miró. Whence your irreconcilable hostility to all of this?

OK: Non-objective art is itself the worst of all our spiritual enemies. Art without vision is hostile to life and hostile to the world. Man is the measure of all things. Whoever uses any other measure, measures falsely.

KOKOSCHKA : A CHRONOLOGY

1886

Born March 1 in the small Austrian town of Pöchlarn on the Danube. Mother from Styria; father from Prague, member of an ancient family of goldsmiths, originally settled in Augsburg, Germany. A few days following Oskar's birth the house in Pöchlarn burns to the ground. Mother and babe (with an elder son) move temporarily in with her brother, who lives in a forest ranger's cottage in Hochkarn. The father runs a jeweller's shop in Prague, where the family dwells in an old patrician house, but they lose everything in the financial crash during the eighties. They move to Vienna, where they are not much better off.

1889–1901

At the time of the move to Vienna, Oskar is about three years old. The father becomes a travelling salesman in the jewellery trade. His work takes him to Paris and other major centres, and he is often away from home for months on end. The mother is compelled to look after herself and her children as best she can, on the slenderest of means. Oskar soon becomes her comfort, which he remains for the rest of her life. There are four children now, but the eldest dies very young (1891). The death of his brother leaves a profound impression on Oskar. (OK told me: 'Death is always astonishing and incomprehensible to a child. I vividly remember everything associated with this death. My mother broke down. I had to suffer through it with her and console her.')

1902–08

Oskar absolves elementary and high school in Vienna. He sings in the choir of the Piarist Church, and during choir practice he receives his first art impressions – the luminous stained-glass windows and the late baroque ceiling frescoes. At eighteen, after graduation, he toys with the idea of becoming a chemist; but such a course of study would have been far too expensive. He wins a scholarship to the Arts and Crafts School (*Kunstgewerbeschule*), entailing a commitment to become a teacher of drawing at a high school. At the school he learns drawing, lithography, bookbinding, ceramics – all manner of crafts except oil painting, which he teaches himself after 1907. After a brief apprenticeship he becomes assistant to his teacher Czeschka. By day he is a student, during the evening courses a teacher. – The spirit of the Vienna *Kunstgewerbeschule* is oriented exclusively toward ornament and decoration. The entire repertoire consists of variations of stylized flowers and leaves. Young OK, like the ancient Florentines really interested only in the human figure, is unable to adapt himself to this vegetative assembly line. What he asks of his students is unheard of at the time – studies of movement, five-minute sketches. Lean acrobats' children, all skin and bones, serve as his models. – His attitude towards the reigning style at the *Kunstgewerbeschule* is matched by his relationship with the Vienna Crafts Studio (*Wiener Werkstätte*), which keeps him busy with commissions from 1907 to 1909, even though he refuses to bow to its geometric-botanical style. For the *Wiener Werkstätte* OK designs postcards, bookplates and bookbindings, and paints fans. All his designs are dominated by the human figure. – The *Wiener Werkstätte* prints his earliest work of poetry, 'The Dreaming Youths' (*Die träumenden Knaben*, text and eight colour lithographs, 1908). OK takes part in the first 'Art Show' (*Kunstschau*), but insists on exemption from any jury vote, a condition that is granted. He exhibits a huge painting in tempera, 'The Dream Bearers' (*Die Traumtragenden*), which draws the admiration of Adolf Loos but is subsequently lost in the cellars of the *Wiener Werkstätte*. The picture, however, gains him the patronage and friendship of Adolf Loos, who 'guided me through heaven and hell of human experience.' – Lotte Franzos, a woman of charm and character, enters his life, and as Loos had introduced him to the world of the spirit, she initiates him into the world of love and of the senses. OK paints her portrait (Plate 1). The oil paints he uses are a gift from Adolf Loos.

1909–10

Crucial to these years, in which OK breaks through to find his own identity, is his relationship with the great Viennese architect Adolf Loos, who openly leads the 'Crusade against Ornament' which Kokoschka has instinctively waged from earliest youth. Loos unmoors the young artist from the *Kunstgewerbeschule* and the *Wiener Werkstätte*, where ornament reigns supreme. He introduces OK to Karl Kraus, master of classical and unadorned prose. Loos secures portrait commissions for his protégé, first in Vienna, then in Switzerland. In the high Alps OK paints a magnificent winter landscape (Plate 3), brimful of light and colour, in terms of technique the point of departure for all his later works, even his portraits. – OK enters into a close association with the Berlin avant-garde periodical *Der Sturm*, its editor, Herwarth Walden, and Walden's wife, Else

Lasker-Schüler, the poet. He moves to Berlin for a year, takes a trip to the Rhineland with the Waldens, and publishes a series of drawings in *Der Sturm* which are decades ahead of art trends in Europe. – First collective show of OK's works at Paul Cassirer's, Berlin. – OK writes plays that are produced and that mark the beginning of the expressionist theatre. Even more than his paintings and drawings, these plays arouse vehement opposition in the conservative-eclectic circles of Vienna. – OK lives in poverty. – Karl Kraus, with his infallible sense of true genius, champions the artist.

1911–14

OK returns from Berlin to Vienna. He again teaches at the *Kunstgewerbeschule*, an evening life class, but instead of using standing or seated models he will have only figures in motion. He illustrates the story *Tubutsch* by Albert Ehrenstein (1911). These twelve pen and ink drawings with their 'prismatic structure' mark a new manner of representation, recurring later in Picasso. Together with the Russian Kandinsky, the Swiss Klee and the German Franz Marc, OK exhibits paintings and drawings at the Gallery *Der Sturm*. – Opposition to OK's stage plays deepens into a scandal, and he loses his teaching post at the *Kunstgewerbeschule*. He next teaches drawing at a Vienna girls' school for a year. He makes the acquaintance of Alma Mahler, widow of the composer Gustav Mahler and seven years his senior, but her vanity and imperious ways constantly cloud the relationship. With her he makes a trip to Venice, where the paintings of Tintoretto and Veronese fire his sense of colour. In the Spring of 1914 he paints 'The Tempest', which he leaves unsigned. (The picture, painted in tempestuous colours, heavy blues and yellows, shows OK and Alma Mahler in a shell-shaped boat without oars or rudder, drifting on the ocean waves. Plate 16.) He presents his companion with six painted fans, documenting the three years of their stormy romance. The last of these fans is a parting gift. The war breaks out, and OK volunteers for the cavalry.

1914–18

OK is severely wounded on the Polish front – a shot in the head and a bayonet stab wound to the lung (September, 1915). He is taken to a military hospital in Vienna, then to another in Dresden. Ill and in pain, he paints, draws, illustrates, resumes his association with the periodical *Der Sturm*, publishes portfolios, exhibits in Berlin. – In September, 1917, exactly two years after being wounded, he is sent to a specialist in Stockholm, but treatment of his head injury remains unsuccessful and he is returned to the military hospital in Dresden. –

In Dresden a new circle of friends has formed around him, including writers and actors. At the Albert Theatre in Dresden three of his plays are produced, designed and staged by himself. He writes 'Orpheus and Eurydice' (1917–18), later turned into an opera by Ernst Křenek (1923). Another of his dramas, 'Murder Hope of Women' (*Mörder Hoffnung der Frauen*), first performed as early as 1908, is published in 1916 in an illustrated edition of *Der Sturm* and put on a year later in the Dada Gallery in Zurich. (Hindemith sets it to music in 1920.)

1918–23

Following demobilization, OK remains in Dresden. – A complete edition of his eleven lithographs to the Bach Cantata is published in 1918. (Begun as early as 1914, nine of them had already appeared in 1916.) – In the Autumn of 1919 OK is appointed professor at the Dresden Academy of Fine Arts. – The Dresden period is one of great productivity. OK paints a number of his most enchanting pictures there – landscapes, figure compositions, many water colours. Nine exhibitions of his works in various cities of Germany during this time.

1924–31

A period of travel: Switzerland, Italy, the Riviera, France, Spain, London, Amsterdam, Berlin. Paris becomes the artist's residence (1924–27), then Auteuil (until 1931). – More travel: North Africa, the Sahara, Egypt; Ireland and Scotland; Istanbul and Jerusalem. In 1930, return to Paris; interludes in Vienna. – Still more travel: Algiers, Italy, Southern Switzerland. The time of greatest productivity. – From 1924 to 1931, twenty-one exhibitions of OK's work are held; he is nevertheless constantly in financial straits. – During this period of feverish travel landscapes predominate in his work, though some important figure paintings and portraits take form as well. The masterpiece among the landscape paintings of the travel years is the great 'Chamonix: Montblanc', with mountain ranges layered like side-scenes on a stage, streaming out infinite light (Plate 30).

1931–38

Once again OK moves to Vienna. Commissioned by the municipality, he paints a landscape with children at play (Plate 36). – Death of his beloved mother (1934). – OK moves to Prague. He paints numerous views of the city, panorama-like, with a marked effect of depth. – OK meets Dr Palkovsky, whose portrait he paints and with whose daughter Olda he becomes friendly. He is commissioned to do a likeness of the President of the

Republic, the philosopher Masaryk. During the sittings the aged statesman discusses with the artist, almost forty years his junior, the philosophy and educational theories of Amos Comenius, whose baroque-humanitarian views OK has admired from his youth. In these hate-filled years from 1935 to 1938 they seem to him to carry special significance – a manifesto for the salvation of Europe. – News of Spanish Civil War atrocities affects OK profoundly, as does the reign of terror that spreads in widening circles in Germany. In 1937 all OK's works are removed from museums and collections as 'degenerate art'. Acts of violence against works of art arouse OK less than those against helpless human beings, crimes that intoxicate the Third Reich as it prepares for war. – In Vienna a great Kokoschka Exhibition is held in 1937, the first in his homeland; but OK is not deceived. He knows that Austria has long since been 'co-ordinated', that her fate is sealed. Immediately after the Munich Pact between Chamberlain and Hitler he foresees the imminent danger to which the Czechoslovak Republic and all other Slavic countries are exposed. He flees to London with his companion Olda Palkovska, later to become his wife.

1939–45

In London his financial situation is desperate. He is without commissions. Virtually the only ones he secures are from Michael Croft (now Lord Croft) and his sister. Soon after the outbreak of war, OK moves to Polperro with his wife Olda; but even there, because of the prevailing suspicion of 'enemy aliens', his situation proves untenable. He is compelled to return to London. During a time of almost daily bombing raids, OK tirelessly paints water-colours of flowers and large canvases of political allegories. – He spends the summer months with his wife in Scotland. – In the time from 1938 to 1945, nine exhibitions of Kokoschka's work are held in America, three in Switzerland and the Netherlands. – He is commissioned to paint the Russian Ambassador in London, Ivan Maisky (Plate 39). The picture's background includes a symbolic hint of the dangers of Russian imperialism, a prophecy that remains unnoticed. OK receives a fee of £1,000 for the Maisky portrait, an enormous sum for him in those days; but he immediately gives it to the Red Cross, for the care of Russian and German soldiers wounded at Stalingrad. – OK's financial state continues at such a low level that he is compelled to scrimp even on canvas and paint; hence most of his works from the war years are water-colours and crayon drawings rather than oil paintings.

1945–52

Immediately after the war Vienna seeks to discharge its great debt to OK by exhibiting two or three dozen of his drawings and water-colours. The exhibition proves nothing to the Viennese, merely demonstrating to people beyond the borders of Austria that the Viennese still do not comprehend their greatest modern painter. In this, OK's first exhibition in Vienna in eight years, his works are hung side by side with hysterical drawings by Schiele, as though the two artists were peers. But henceforth, to the present day, Kokoschka shows in Europe and America tread on each others' heels. – In 1947 Kokoschka becomes a British subject. Brief visits to Switzerland, Italy, Salzburg, Munich, Cologne and Hamburg follow. In 1949 OK is a visiting professor in Boston. In Vienna, that same year, he paints Dr Theodor Körner, the most high-minded and selfless Lord Mayor the city has ever known. Other portraits are painted in Hamburg, London, Switzerland, and – the fruit of his brief journeys – spacious mountain landscapes and city views. In 1950 OK paints his first great mythological composition, 'The Prometheus Saga'.

1953–55

At the summer seminar of the Salzburg Academy, OK runs his 'School of Seeing'. He moves to Switzerland with his wife Olda, settling in Villeneuve on Lake Geneva. The year 1954 sees the creation of his second great mythological composition, 'Thermopylae' (Plates 42–44). At the same time he resumes the designing of stage scenery and costumes (e.g. Mozart's 'Magic Flute' at the Salzburg Festival, and three magic plays by Raimund at the Vienna *Burgtheater*. In 1955 he finishes his design for the tapestry 'Amor and Psyche'.

Since 1956

OK's seventieth birthday and his journey to Greece mark a new era in his creative work. The art of Greece, which has always played a significant role in his imagination, now reigns supreme. Another journey to Greece follows in 1961. The monumental paintings on which he is presently working in Villeneuve testify to the overpowering impression the landscape and the art of Greece have left on him. He has, moreover, again turned to lithography and is now producing more drawings than for many years. (1963: Seventeen lithographs to Shakespeare's 'King Lear'; and stage designs for Verdi's opera 'The Masked Ball', performed in Florence.) – Surprises may be in store for us.

"*The composer takes the essence of his art from within himself —
no one even dreams of suspecting him of imitation; but as for the
painter, nature in plain sight about him seems to be forever ahead
of him, serving as an unattainable paradigm; yet in truth the
painter's art arises quite as spontaneously, quite as much* a priori
*as the composer's; the only difference being that the painter employs
a symbolic language infinitely more complex. The painter, in truth,
paints with his eyes . . . His vision is all action — action that is
itself creative. His pictures are no more than his private code, his
means of expression, his instrument of representation. One may
well compare this code to musical notation.*" Novalis, about 1798.

PLATES

1. PORTRAIT OF LOTTE FRANZOS. 1908–9. Washington, Phillips Collection

2. Portrait of Adolf Loos. 1909. Berlin-Charlottenburg, National Gallery

3. Dent du Midi. 1909. Zurich, Marianne Feilchenfeldt Collection

4. PORTRAIT OF THE MARQUIS DE MONTESQUIEU. 1909–10. Stockholm, National Museum

5. PORTRAIT OF THE MARQUISE
DE ROHAN-MONTESQUIEU.
1909–10. Rome,
Mr. and Mrs. Paul E. Geier Collection

6. PORTRAIT OF AUGUSTE FOREL. 1910. Mannheim, Kunsthalle

7. PORTRAIT OF ELSE KUPFER. 1910–11. Zurich, Kunsthaus

8. KNIGHT, DEATH AND ANGEL. 1910–11. Zurich, Hans C. Bechtler Collection

9. CRUCIFIXION. 1911. Zurich, Hans C. Bechtler Collection

10. Portrait of Baron Victor von Dirsztay. 1911. Hanover, Dr. B. Sprengel Collection

11. DOUBLE PORTRAIT: OSKAR KOKOSCHKA AND ALMA MAHLER. 1912. Hamburg, Prof. E. Horstmann Collection

13. SELF-PORTRAIT, POINTING TO THE BREAST. 1913.
New York, Museum of Modern Art

14. Dolomite Landscape: Tre Croci. 1913. Hamburg, Prof. E. Horstmann Collection

15. Detail from Plate 14

16. THE TEMPEST.
1914. Basle, Kunstmuseum

18. STOCKHOLM HARBOUR. 1917. Hamburg, Prof. E. Horstmann Collection

19. THE POWER OF MUSIC. 1918–19. Eindhoven, Stedelijk Museum

20. PORTRAIT OF GITTA WALLERSTEIN. About 1921. Stuttgart, Willy Hahn Collection

21. PARIS: THE ROOF OF THE OPERA. 1924. Hamburg, Prof. E. Horstmann Collection

22. Dresden: Augustus Bridge with Steamer. 1923. Eindhoven, Stedelijk Museum

23. FLORENCE: BANKS OF THE ARNO. 1924. Hanover, Dr. B. Sprengel Collection

24. Portrait of Ernst Blass. 1925. Bremen, Kunsthalle

25. Portrait of Karl Kraus. 1925. Vienna, Museum of Twentieth-Century Art

26. THE TIGON. 1926. New York, Museum of Modern Art

27. THE MANDRILL. 1926. Rotterdam, Museum Boymans-Van Beuningen

28. Richmond Terrace. 1926. Berne, Dr. Gysin Collection

29. LONDON: LARGE THAMES VIEW. 1926. Buffalo (N.Y.), Albright Art Gallery

30. Chamonix: Montblanc. 1927. Karlsruhe, Kunsthalle

31. Detail from Plate 30

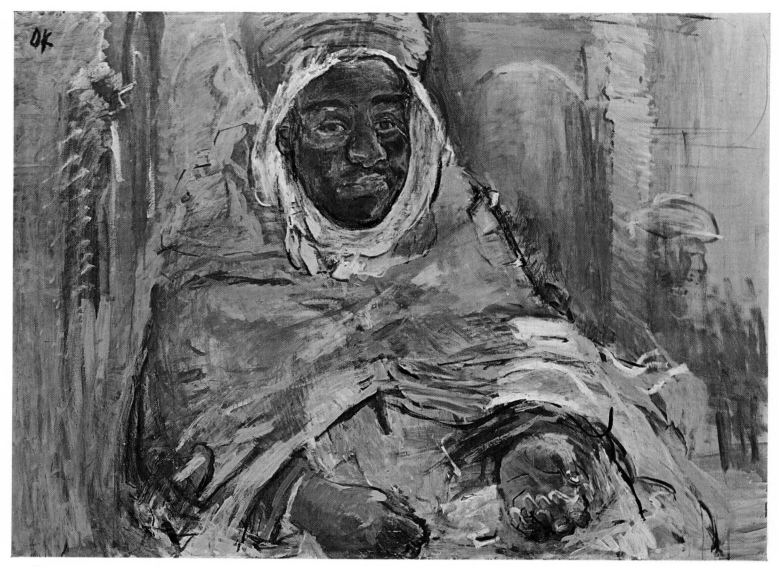

32. PORTRAIT OF THE MARABOUT OF TEMACINE (Sidi Ahmet Ben Tidjani). 1928. Hamburg, Prof. E. Horstmann Collection

33. PORTRAIT OF MARCEL VON NEMES. 1929. Linz, Neue Galerie

34. TUNIS MARKET. 1928–29. London, Private Collection

35. JERUSALEM. 1929–30. Detroit, Institute of Arts

36. VIENNA: VIEW FROM THE WILHELMINENBERG. 1931. Vienna, Historisches Museum

37. Prague: Charles Bridge (with Boat). 1934. Prague, National Gallery

38. MOTHER AND CHILD (IN THE GARDEN). 1934. London, Marlborough Fine Art Ltd.

39. PORTRAIT OF AMBASSADOR IVAN MAISKY. 1942–43. London, Tate Gallery

40. FLORENCE CATHEDRAL. 1948. Los Angeles, Donald Winston Collection

41. MALOJA. 1951. Stuttgart, Willy Hahn Collection

42. THERMOPYLAE I: THE DEPARTURE OF LEONIDAS. 1954. Hamburg, Hochschulbehörde

43. THERMOPYLAE II: THE BARBARIANS. 1954. Hamburg, Hochschulbehörde

44. THERMOPYLAE III: THE BATTLE. 1954. Hamburg, Hochschulbehörde

45. DELPHI. 1956. Hanover, Gallery

46. Vienna, State Opera. 1956. Vienna, Oesterreichische Galerie

47. LÜBECK: JAKOBIKIRCHE. 1958. Lübeck, Behnhaus

48. HERODOTUS. 1960–1963. (Unfinished.) In the artist's possession

NOTES TO THE PLATES

All the paintings here reproduced are painted in oil on canvas and signed, except for No. 16, which is unsigned, and the 'Thermopylae triptych', which is painted in tempera (No. 42–44).

'W' refers to the oeuvre catalogue (1906–1956) in *Oskar Kokoschka: The Work of the Painter*, by H. M. Wingler, London, 1958.

OSKAR KOKOSCHKA AND HIS WIFE OLDA. 1961–63 (unfinished). In the artist's studio at Villeneuve.

NOTES TO THE PLATES

RECORDED BY OLDA KOKOSCHKA
FROM REMARKS MADE BY HER HUSBAND

1. PORTRAIT OF LOTTE FRANZOS. (W.11) $44\frac{7}{8} \times 31\frac{1}{2}$ inches. Washington, Phillips Collection.

'The first portrait of a woman I ever painted. I was in love with painting, and with the girl – that's the reason the picture is painted so tenderly. I spent a long time working on it, beginning in the Summer of 1908, to the end of the year, and probably into the next. I was still working with the *Wiener Werkstätte* and the *Kunstgewerbeschule* at the time – but not very much longer.'

2. PORTRAIT OF ADOLF LOOS. (W.15) $29\frac{1}{8} \times 36\frac{5}{8}$ inches. Berlin–Charlottenburg, National Gallery.

'Loos was my Virgil, who led me through heaven and hell of human experience.'

'I met him in 1908, and a year later, when I was already free of the *Wiener Werkstätte*, I painted him. I once thought Loos himself had put the year 1909 on his portrait, but I now remember clearly, I did it myself. Loos didn't have any oil paints. At any rate, the year wasn't painted on the picture until a year or two afterwards.'

3. DENT DU MIDI. (W.30) $29\frac{7}{8} \times 45\frac{5}{8}$ inches. Zurich, Mrs. Marianne Feilchenfeldt.

'In the winter of 1909 Loos took me to Switzerland – you can see him in the foreground, on the sleigh, riding off. It was the first time I was abroad, my first time in the mountains, which I had known before only from the posters of the travel agencies. There were the snow and the mountains and the light, and I was alone – and that is what I painted.'

4. PORTRAIT OF THE MARQUIS DE MONTESQUIEU. (W.34) $31\frac{1}{8} \times 24\frac{3}{4}$ inches. Stockholm, National Museum.

'In 1909, before Christmas, Loos took me to Leysin in Switzerland, to a tuberculosis sanatorium, with a view of the Dent du Midi. I painted Mrs. Loos there, her name was Bessie, and then, a bit later, Conte Verona, and the Marquis de Montesquieu and his wife – people at death's door, all of them. I was very fond of the Marquise.'

5. PORTRAIT OF THE MARQUISE DE ROHAN-MONTESQUIEU. (W.33) $37\frac{3}{8} \times 19\frac{3}{4}$ inches. Rome, Mr. and Mrs. Paul E. Geier.

See Note to No. 4.

6. PORTRAIT OF AUGUSTE FOREL. (W.36) $28 \times 22\frac{7}{8}$ inches. Mannheim, Kunsthalle.

'I painted this portrait of the famous Swiss biologist and sexologist at Yvorne in Switzerland, in January 1910. In the summer of that year it was shown at Paul Cassirer's in Berlin.'

'It was painted during the winter evenings by lamplight. The learned man's family sat about, and I listened to their conversation, which made me blush – until I discovered that they were talking about the sex life of ants.'

7. PORTRAIT OF ELSE KUPFER. (W.49) $35\frac{1}{2} \times 28$ inches. Zurich, Kunsthaus.

'She was an actress and a very amorous lady, who had a host of admirers in Vienna.'

'I was then just engaged in discovering how a person's character may be expressed through colour.'

8. KNIGHT, DEATH AND ANGEL. Second Version. Dated 1910. (W.48) $33\frac{1}{4} \times 29\frac{1}{2}$ inches. Zurich, Hans C. Bechtler.

'The first version of this picture was, I believe, my first religious composition. And I painted it for my mother. That is, I painted it twice – the first version was sold, because I needed the money, and then I painted it again, from memory.'

9. CRUCIFIXION. (W.53) $22 \times 27\frac{1}{8}$ inches. Zurich, Hans C. Bechtler.

'I painted the picture in 1911, in Vienna. It is one of my first efforts with a composition of several figures, and I used the interplay of colours I had learned in portrait painting before.'

10. PORTRAIT OF BARON VICTOR VON DIRSZTAY. (W.56) $38\frac{5}{8} \times 28\frac{3}{4}$ inches. Hanover, Dr Bernhard Sprengel.

'I painted him and his nephew, and I illustrated two books he wrote.'

11. DOUBLE PORTRAIT: OSKAR KOKOSCHKA AND ALMA MAHLER. (W.71) $39\frac{3}{8} \times 35\frac{1}{2}$ inches. Hamburg, Professor Edgar Horstmann.

'One of my earliest self-portraits – a highly personal page in my autobiography, painted at a critical phase of my life.'

12. GIRL WITH PEKINESE. (W.74) 37×28 inches. Mannheim, Kunsthalle.

'The picture is a repetition of another I painted in 1912 or 1913, which I liked much better. Unfortunately it has been lost. The colours of the first version were much better.'

13. SELF-PORTRAIT, POINTING TO THE BREAST. (W.72) $31\frac{7}{8}$×$19\frac{3}{4}$ inches. New York, Museum of Modern Art.

'A variation in blue. Red and the other colours are very sparingly used.'

14. DOLOMITE LANDSCAPE: TRE CROCI. (W.81) $32\frac{1}{4}$×$46\frac{7}{8}$ inches. Hamburg, Professor Edgar Horstmann.

'An attempt to represent space through the luminosity of vivid colours.'

15. DETAIL FROM PLATE 14, ORIGINAL SIZE.

16. THE TEMPEST. (W.96). Unsigned. $71\frac{1}{4}$×$86\frac{5}{8}$ inches. Basel, Kunstmuseum.

'My most ambitious composition from this period. It is purposely unsigned. It was finished in the Spring of 1914 and was exhibited at the Munich Secessionist show in May. I sold it then, and the money I got for it was enough to buy a horse, which I needed, since soon afterward I joined the Dragoons in the war.'

17. LOVERS WITH CAT. (W.116) $36\frac{5}{8}$×$51\frac{1}{4}$ inches. Zurich, Kunsthaus.

'In Dresden, in 1917, my plays, "Murder Hope of Women", "The Burning Bush", and "Job" were performed. I directed myself. Käthe Richter, whom I drew and painted repeatedly afterwards, played leading roles in these performances. Behind the actress one sees Walter Hasenclever, author of "Antigone".'

18. STOCKHOLM HARBOUR. (W.118) $37\frac{3}{4}$×$49\frac{5}{8}$ inches. Hamburg, Professor Edgar Horstmann.

'In September 1915 I was gravely wounded at the front in Poland, and I still felt the effects two years later. The Austrian Army sent me from Dresden to Stockholm, where a specialist for my kind of injury was treating Austrian soldiers – my case was of interest to the high command. But the specialist didn't accomplish anything. It was at this time, in the Autumn of 1917 that I painted the harbour in Stockholm. Then I was ordered back to Dresden and the military hospital there.'

19. THE POWER OF MUSIC. (W.130) $40\frac{1}{8}$×59 inches. Eindhoven, Stedelijk Museum.

'In this composition, I think, I had my greatest success in keeping the colours so luminous that they glow like stained-glass windows.'

20. PORTRAIT OF GITTA WALLERSTEIN. (W.139) $33\frac{1}{2}$×$23\frac{5}{8}$ inches. Stuttgart, Willy Hahn.

'The daughter of a friend of mine, Dr Victor Wallerstein, whose portrait I also painted. In that same year, 1921, he wrote in a Berlin art journal about the pictures I had then painted most recently.'

21. PARIS: THE ROOF OF THE OPERA. (W.174) $25\frac{5}{8}$×$19\frac{3}{4}$ inches. Hamburg, Professor Edgar Horstmann.

'Painted late one evening from the window of my room, very quickly, during a storm.'

22. DRESDEN: AUGUSTUS BRIDGE WITH STEAMER. (W.155) $25\frac{5}{8}$×$37\frac{3}{8}$ inches. Eindhoven, Stedelijk Museum.

'I repeatedly painted this view of the city with the landing-place for ships and the Augustus Bridge, always in different lighting. What interested me in it was the rhythmic tension of the bridge arches across the broad, agitated surface of the water.'

23. FLORENCE: BANKS OF THE ARNO. (W.168) $27\frac{1}{2}$×$39\frac{3}{8}$ inches. Hanover, Dr Bernhard Sprengel.

'A thinly painted oil sketch. In the Spring of 1924 I was in Italy with Paul Cassirer, the Berlin art dealer. Then, in the Autumn, I was in Paris with Loos.'

24. PORTRAIT OF ERNST BLASS. (W.207) $31\frac{1}{2}$×$47\frac{1}{4}$ inches. Bremen, Kunsthalle.

'I painted the picture in 1925 in Berlin. Blass, at twenty-two, published some beautiful lyric poems. Later he contracted a dreadful illness and went blind. In my painting I tried to show his blindness quite plainly, because it moved me deeply.'

25. PORTRAIT OF KARL KRAUS. (W.180) $25\frac{5}{8}$×$39\frac{3}{8}$ inches. Vienna, Museum of the Twentieth Century.

'Karl Kraus, the great satirist, is known to have worked by night and slept by day. That is why I painted an electric light bulb and a nocturnal butterfly into the background of his portrait.'

26. THE TIGON. (W.216) $37\frac{3}{4}$×$49\frac{5}{8}$ inches. New York, Museum of Modern Art.

'Through Julian Huxley, at that time Director of the London Zoo, I got permission to paint the animals undisturbed, early in the morning, before visiting hours.

When I was face to face with the tigon, nature's weird and inventive imagination made a deep impression on me.'

27. THE MANDRILL. (W.215) $50\times39\frac{3}{4}$ inches. Rotterdam, Museum Boymans-van Beuningen.

'When I painted him, I saw: that's a wild, isolated fellow, almost a mirror image of me. One who wants to be left alone.'

28. RICHMOND TERRACE. (W.218) $35\frac{1}{2}\times51\frac{1}{4}$ inches. Berne, Dr Gysin.

'Painted on sunny Summer afternoons. What I tried here was to express space and spatial depth through various shades of blue – that never come out right in reproduction.'

29. LONDON: LARGE THAMES VIEW. (W.208) $35\frac{1}{2}\times51\frac{1}{4}$ inches. Buffalo (New York), Albright Art Gallery.

'I never grew tired of painting the Thames. This landscape is from the year 1926, from the roof of the old Cecil Hotel. Today the view is quite different. The new "South Bank Architecture" has changed it completely. Two other Thames landscapes I painted before the Second World War have been lost in France without a trace. Today not one of my pictures hangs in a French collection! In the year 1954 I painted the Thames once again.'

30. CHAMONIX: MONTBLANC. (W.230) $35\frac{1}{2}\times51\frac{1}{4}$ inches. Karlsruhe, Kunsthalle.

'The colourful richness of old brocade, combined with a structure of numerous planes, guiding the eye from depth to depth.'

31. DETAIL FROM PLATE 30, ONE-HALF ORIGINAL SIZE.

32. PORTRAIT OF THE MARABOUT OF TEMACINE. (W.237) $38\frac{1}{4}\times51\frac{1}{4}$ inches. Hamburg, Professor Edgar Horstmann.

'Head of a Mohammedan sect. I enjoyed his hospitality during the month of fasting, Ramadan. His residence was like a beehive. Pilgrims from many African oases came to him, to plead for cure and blessing. The picture is painted in the colours of the Arabian desert.'

33. PORTRAIT OF MARCEL VON NEMES. (W.245) $53\frac{1}{8}\times37\frac{3}{8}$ inches. Linz, Neue Galerie.

'He was a well-known Hungarian art collector who lived in Munich. He owned many paintings by El Greco, and he restored them himself. I had known him since 1910. I painted him in 1929.'

34. TUNIS MARKET. (W.233) $33\frac{7}{8}\times50\frac{3}{4}$ inches. London, Private collection.

'An Arab city full of noise, teeming, ant-like, with people busy at their trades and shops. Painted from the roof of an Arab greengrocer's house.'

35. JERUSALEM. (W.244) $31\frac{1}{2}\times50\frac{3}{4}$ inches. Detroit, Institute of Arts.

'An ancient city, in hot light, surrounded by a huge wall, parts of which go back to the Bible age. In the foreground oxen that look like rocks. All of this is reproduced on a canvas of moderate size.'

36. VIENNA: VIEW FROM THE WILHELMINENBERG. (W.260) $36\frac{1}{4}\times53\frac{1}{2}$ inches. Vienna, Historisches Museum.

'A commission from the Vienna City Council, on the occasion of the founding of a large children's home on the Wilhelminenberg. I then lived in Liebhartstal, not very far away. The city is seen in the background and in the extreme distance is the Danube. The whole wide foreground is full of children at play.'

37. PRAGUE: CHARLES BRIDGE (WITH BOAT). (W.289) $34\frac{1}{4}\times48$ inches. Prague, National Gallery.

'I repeatedly painted Prague and the Vltava, almost as often as Dresden and the Elbe, and London and the Thames.'

38. MOTHER AND CHILD (IN THE GARDEN). (W.281) $22\frac{1}{8}\times29\frac{1}{2}$ inches. London, Marlborough Fine Art Ltd.

'The model for the "mother" was Trudl, who was then fourteen. I often drew and painted her on other occasions. She was a neighbour's child. And the model for the baby was a doll. This is the last picture I painted of Trudl, in 1934, before I moved to Prague.'

39. PORTRAIT OF AMBASSADOR IVAN MAISKY. (W.328) $47\frac{1}{4}\times29\frac{7}{8}$ inches. London, Tate Gallery.

'He was Russian Ambassador in London at the time. He read *The Times* while I painted him. As a test of people's vigilance, I painted Lenin in the background, pointing to a globe on which nothing can be seen but the Russian Empire. But nobody noticed it.'

40. FLORENCE CATHEDRAL. (W.352) $37\frac{3}{4}\times49\frac{1}{4}$ inches. Los Angeles, Donald Winston.

'Painted from the roof of a loggia on the cathedral square.'

'My personal contribution to the vogue for cubism. The

structure is broken down into hundreds of facets, each with its own colour. This was to show how to go about letting colour rather than geometry determine a picture.'

41. MALOJA. (W.372) $25\frac{5}{8} \times 31\frac{7}{8}$ inches. Stuttgart, Willy Hahn.

'Painted in the Engadine, on the way to Italy, in September, 1951.'

42–44. THERMOPYLAE. (W.384–386). Triptych. Overall size, $88\frac{5}{8} \times 315$ inches. (The side panels, Plates 42 and 43, are $88\frac{5}{8} \times 98\frac{3}{8}$ inches; the centre panel is $88\frac{5}{8} \times 118\frac{1}{8}$ inches.) Tempera on canvas. Hamburg, Board of Higher Education.

'I painted these three pictures from the Winter of 1953 to the Winter of 1954. A year later I published an essay on the content of the pictures. People will simply have to read that, for it cannot be said in a shorter space.'

45. DELPHI. (W.393) $31\frac{7}{8} \times 45\frac{1}{4}$ inches. Hanover, Gallery of Lower Saxony.

'Painted in the Spring of 1956. My first great impression of the Greek mountain landscape.'

46. VIENNA: STATE OPERA. (W.394) $32\frac{1}{4} \times 45\frac{1}{4}$ inches. Vienna, Österreichische Galerie.

'Painted in June 1956, soon after my return from Greece.'
'Opposite the Opera was an unfinished building, where I set up my easel and painted at night, while they played and sang opera inside and the structure was brilliantly illuminated from the outside by searchlights.'

47. LÜBECK: JACOBIKIRCHE. $31\frac{1}{2} \times 43\frac{1}{4}$ inches. Lübeck, Behnhaus.

'At the time, mid-summer of 1958, I was living in Travemünde. I painted the church from the window of a residence that belonged to friends. The light was brilliant.'

48. HERODOTUS. $71 \times 47\frac{1}{4}$ inches. In the possession of the artist.

'The painting comes close to being a repetition of the large figure in the lower left corner of the centre panel of the "Thermopylae" triptych (Plate 44). I began the picture on New Year's Day 1960. It isn't quite finished yet.'

Plate I: SELF-PORTRAIT, 1912. Detail from Plate 11, two-thirds the size of the original.

Plate II: THE SPIRE OF ST. STEPHEN'S IN VIENNA. Detail from Plate 46, original size.

Plate III: COUNTRY HOUSE OF THE GEM-DEALER ROSSI. Coloured chalks, drawing on paper. Dated 1959. $20\frac{1}{8} \times 25\frac{1}{4}$ inches. In the possession of the artist.

'When I was young, I always designed the settings for my own plays and directed them as well. Later I designed the stage decorations for the three magic plays by Ferdinand Raimund, for the *Burgtheater* productions in 1960, 1961 and 1962. The drawing, "The Country House of the Gem-Dealer", was intended for the second act of "Moisasur's Magic Curse". Only the door on the left and the niche on the right were solid. Everything else was painted on the backcloth.

The paintings are reproduced with kind permission of the Stuttgarter Kunstkabinett.

LIST OF COLLECTIONS

BASEL, Kunstmuseum
  The Tempest, 16

BERLIN-DAHLEM, Former State Museums
  Portrait of Adolf Loos, 2

BERNE, Dr Gysin
  Richmond Terrace, 28

BREMEN, Kunsthalle
  Portrait of Ernst Blass, 24

BUFFALO (New York), Albright Art Gallery
  London: Large Thames View, 29

DETROIT, Institute of Art
  Jerusalem, 35

EINDHOVEN, Stedelijk Museum
  The Power of Music, 19
  Dresden: Augustus Bridge with Steamer, 22

HAMBURG, Board of Higher Education
  Thermopylae Triptych, 42–44

HAMBURG, Prof. Edgar Horstmann
  Oskar Kokoschka and Alma Mahler, 11, and I
  Dolomite Landscape: Tre Croci, 14–15
  Stockholm Harbour, 18
  Paris: The Roof of the Opera, 21
  Portrait of the Marabout of Temacine, 32

HANOVER, Gallery of Lower Saxony
  Delphi, 45

HANOVER, Dr Bernhard Sprengel
  Portrait of Baron Victor von Dirsztay, 10
  Florence: Banks of the Arno, 23

KARLSRUHE, Kunsthalle.
  Chamonix: Montblanc, 30–31

LINZ, Neue Galerie.
  Portrait of Marcel von Nemes, 33

LONDON, Tate Gallery
  Portrait of Ambassador Ivan Maisky, 39

LONDON, Marlborough Fine Art Ltd.
  Mother and Child (In the Garden), 38

LONDON, Marlborough Fine Art Ltd.
  Tunis Market, 34

LOS ANGELES, Donald Winston
  Florence Cathedral, 40

LÜBECK, Behnhaus
  Lübeck: Jacobikirche, 47

MANNHEIM, Kunsthalle
  Portrait of Auguste Forel, 6
  Girl with Pekinese, 12

NEW YORK, Museum of Modern Art
  Self-Portrait, Pointing to the Breast, 13
  The Tigon, 26

PRAGUE, National Gallery
  Prague: Charles Bridge (with Boat), 37

ROME, Mr. and Mrs. Paul E. Geier
  Portrait of the Marquise de Rohan-Montesquieu, 5

ROTTERDAM, Museum Boymans/Van Beuningen
  The Mandrill, 27

STOCKHOLM, National Museum
  Portrait of the Marquis de Montesquieu, 4

STUTTGART, Willy Hahn
  Portrait of Gitta Wallerstein, 20
  Maloja, 41

VIENNA, Museum of the Twentieth Century
  Portrait of Karl Kraus, 25

VIENNA, Historisches Museum
  Vienna: View from the Wilheminenberg, 36

VIENNA, Österreichische Galerie
  Vienna, State Opera, 46 and II

VILLENEUVE, Oskar Kokoschka
  Herodotus, 48
  Country House of the Gem-Dealer Rossi, III

WASHINGTON, Phillips Collection
  Portrait of Lotte Franzos, 1

ZURICH, Kunsthaus
  Portrait of Else Kupfer, 7
  Lovers with Cat, 17

ZURICH, Hans C. Bechtler
  Knight, Death and Angel, 8
  Crucifixion, 9

ZURICH, Mrs. Marianne Feilchenfeldt
  Dent du Midi, 3